by Sarina Simon

To Anthony, Daniela, Lenay, Micaela, and Rocket and to all children, who inspire us and give us so much joy.

Printed in the United States of America
First Printing, 2016

ISBN 978-0-9979108-1-0

Comments or Questions?
Contact Us:
Phone: (323) 874-1432
Email: ABCAnimals@northsouthstudios.com

Tips for Parents, Grandparents and Other Caregivers

Chances are you already know that children love to cuddle up and read with their special grownups. These tips will help you make reading together even more exciting as you explore this book with its magic blend of printed words, spoken audio and video.

1. Download the free ABC Animals app at the Apple App Store or Google Play.
2. Read and follow the simple app directions carefully.
3. Sit with your child in a well-lit location.
4. For each letter, read the left hand page aloud and discuss the illustration together. You may also want to point out the key letters on the page.
5. Next, read the question on the corresponding right hand page.
6. Place your device at a distance of about 10 inches from the book.
7. Point the device (camera) at the photograph of the animal on the right hand page.
8. Watch and listen as the animals come alive and the question is answered.
9. If you do not have your device handy and would like to answer the questions yourself, you will find the answers on page 54 of this book.

We hope you enjoy this special reading experience.
If you have any questions or comments, please email us at ABCAnimals@northsouthstudios.com

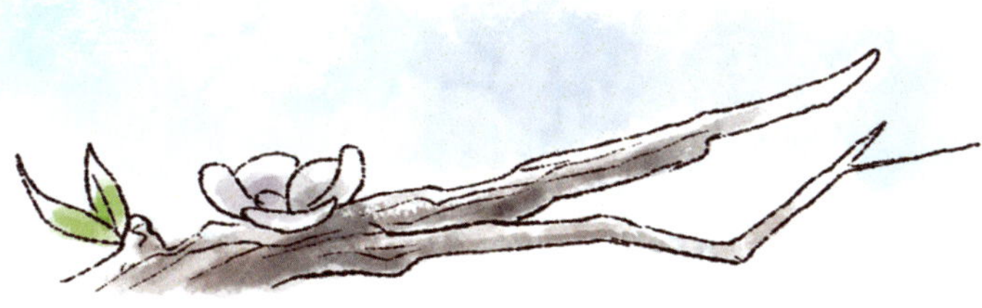

Aa

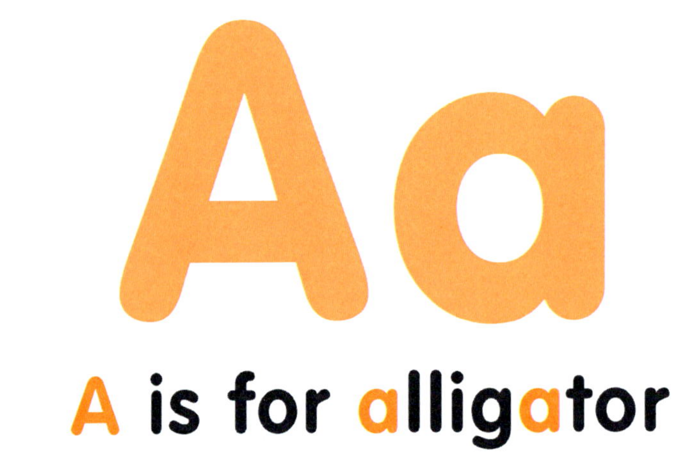

A is for alligator

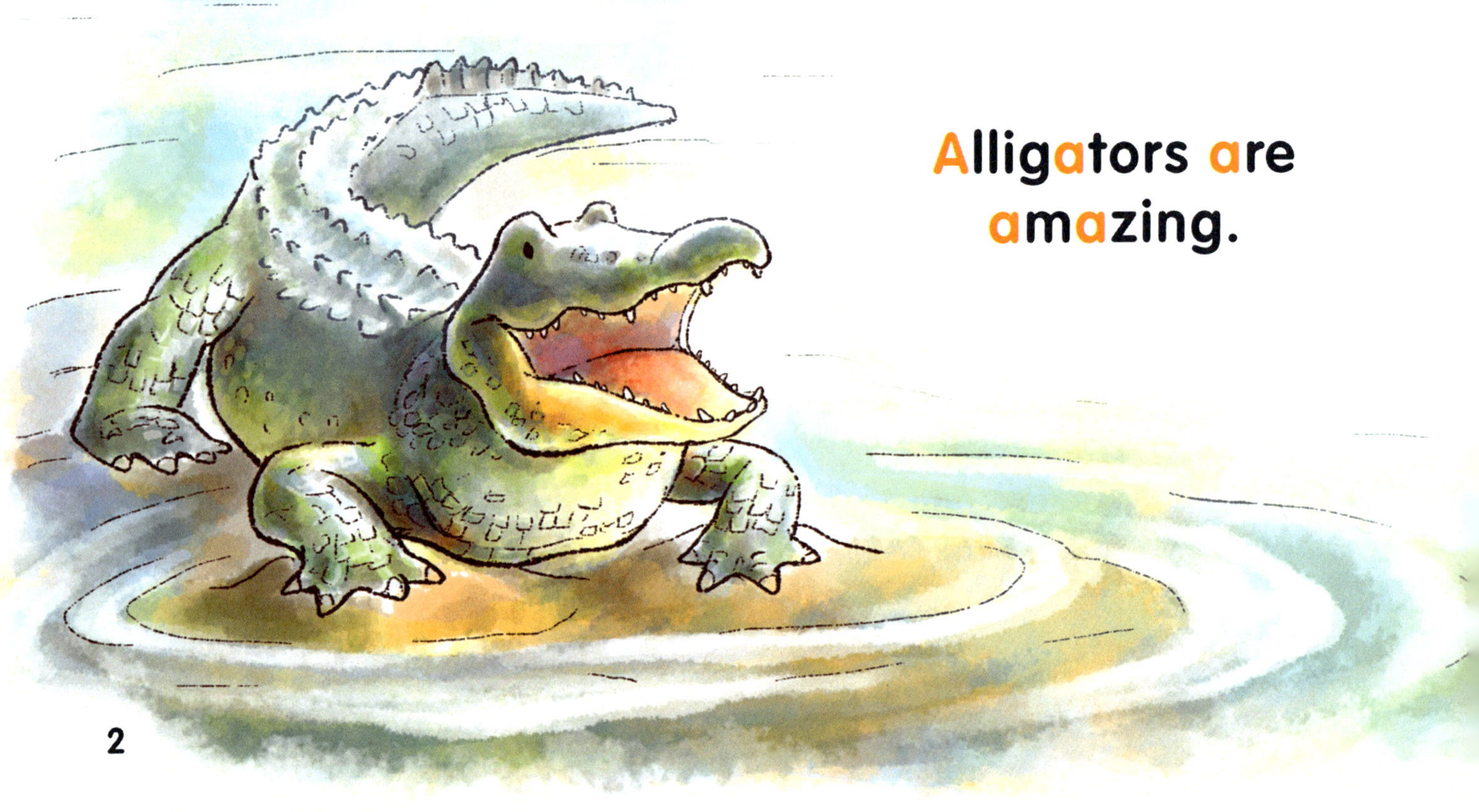

Alligators are
amazing.

How do alligators move?

Bb

B is for bear

Bears eat berries.

What do you call a baby bear?

Cc

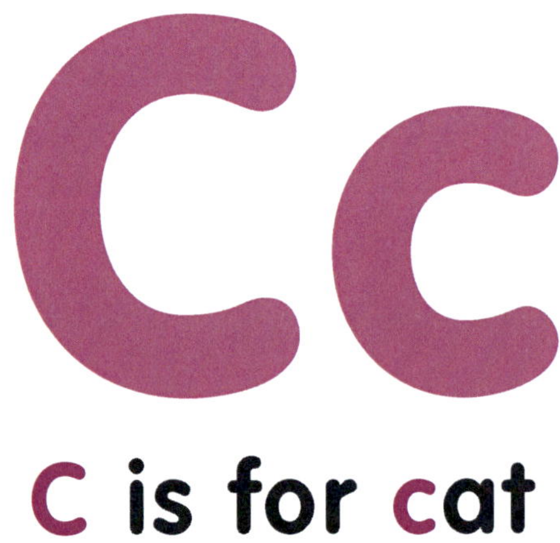

C is for cat

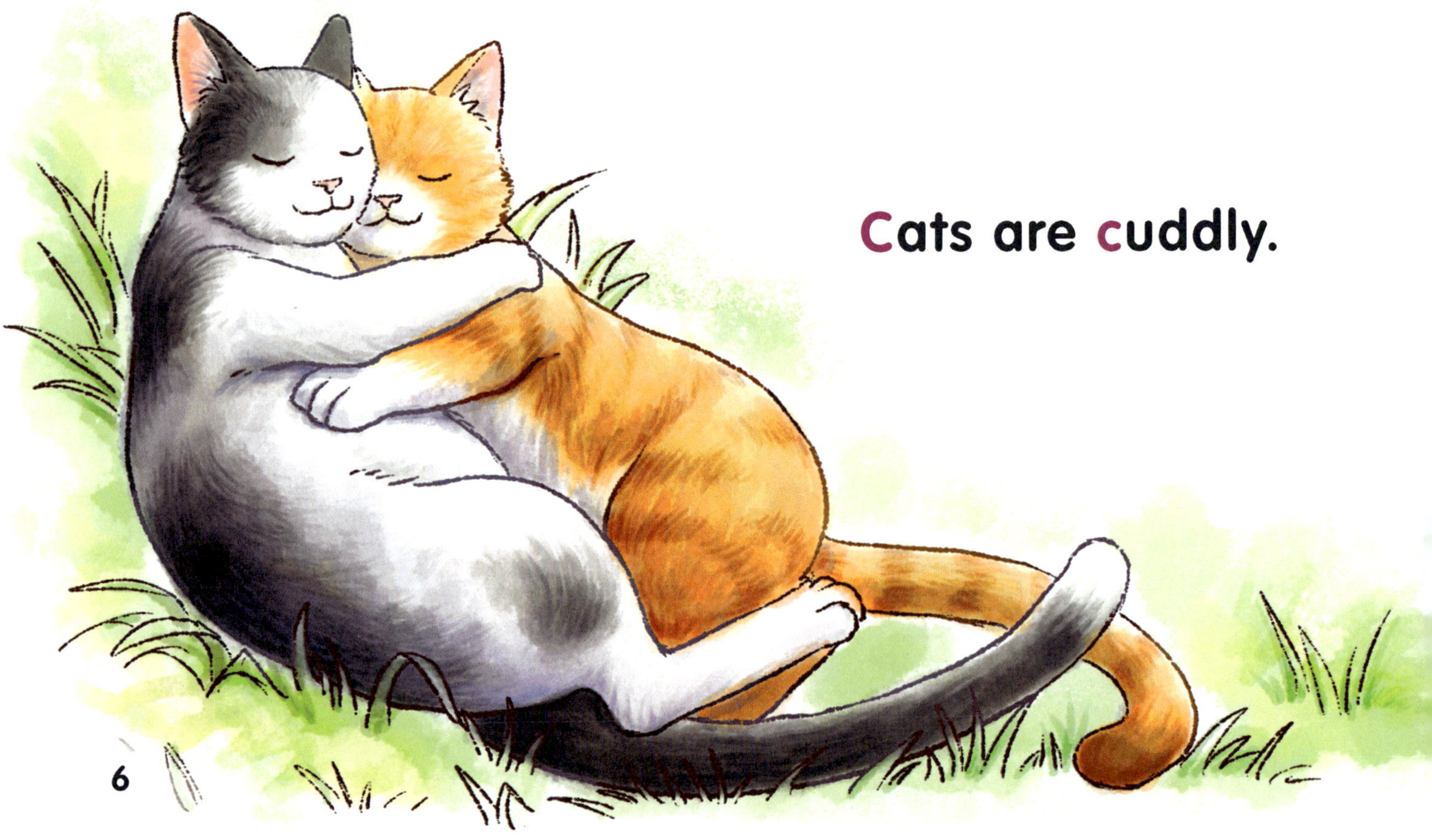

Cats are cuddly.

How do cats clean themselves?

Dd

D is for duck

Ducks like to
dive.

What do you call a baby duck?

Ee

E is for elephant

Elephants are enormous.

What do elephants like to eat?

Ff

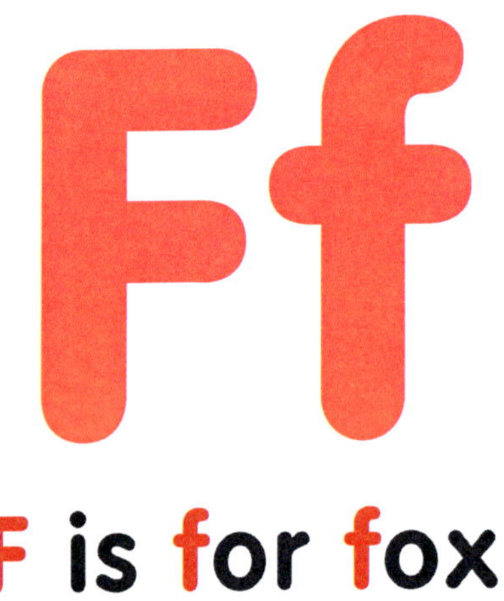

F is for fox

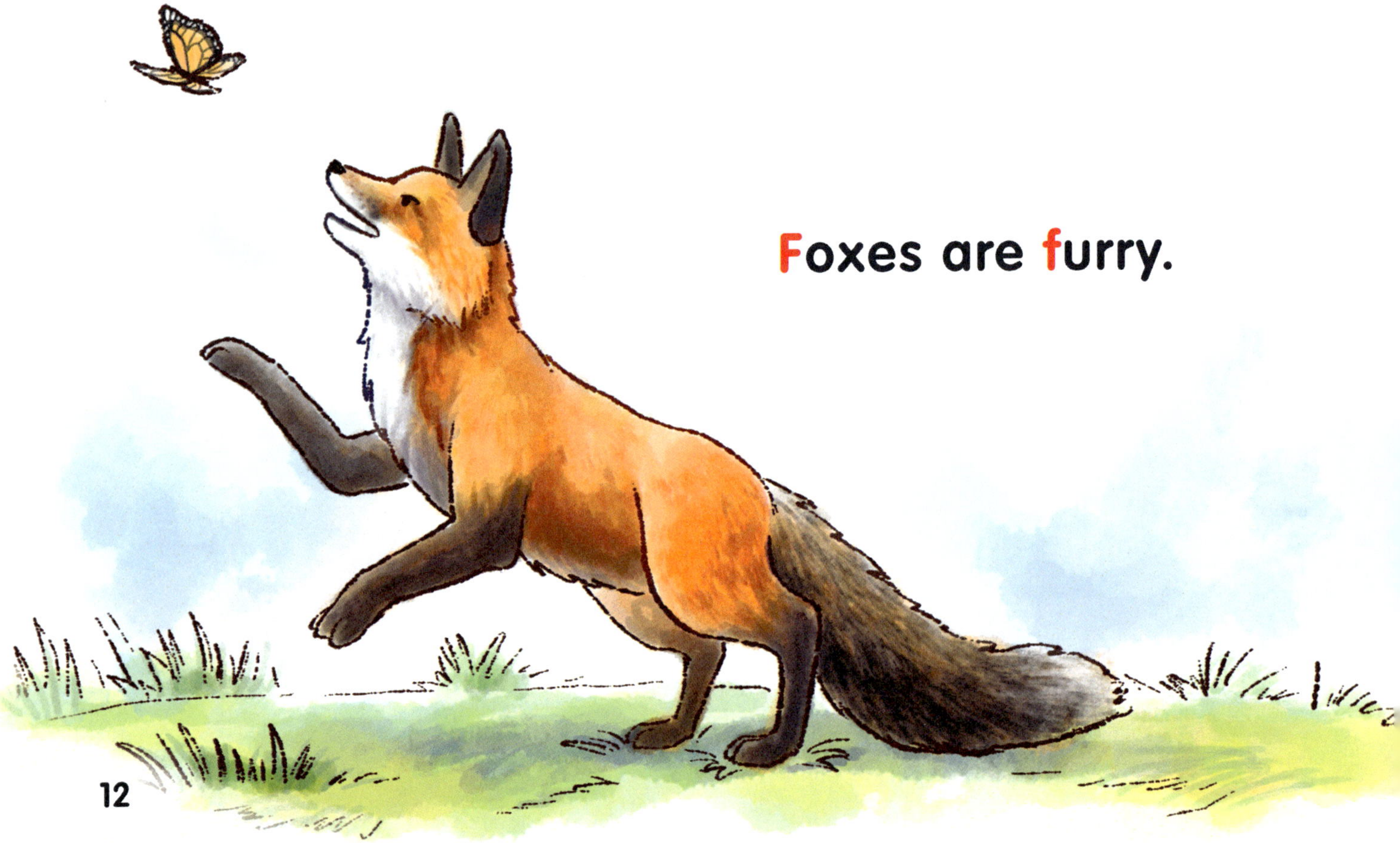

Foxes are furry.

What do you call a baby fox?

Gg

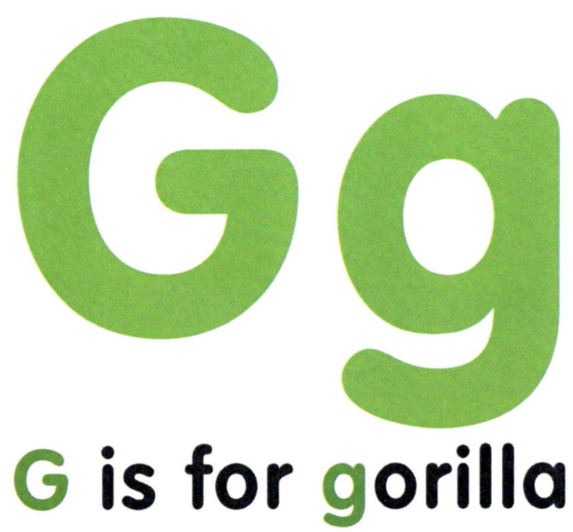

G is for gorilla

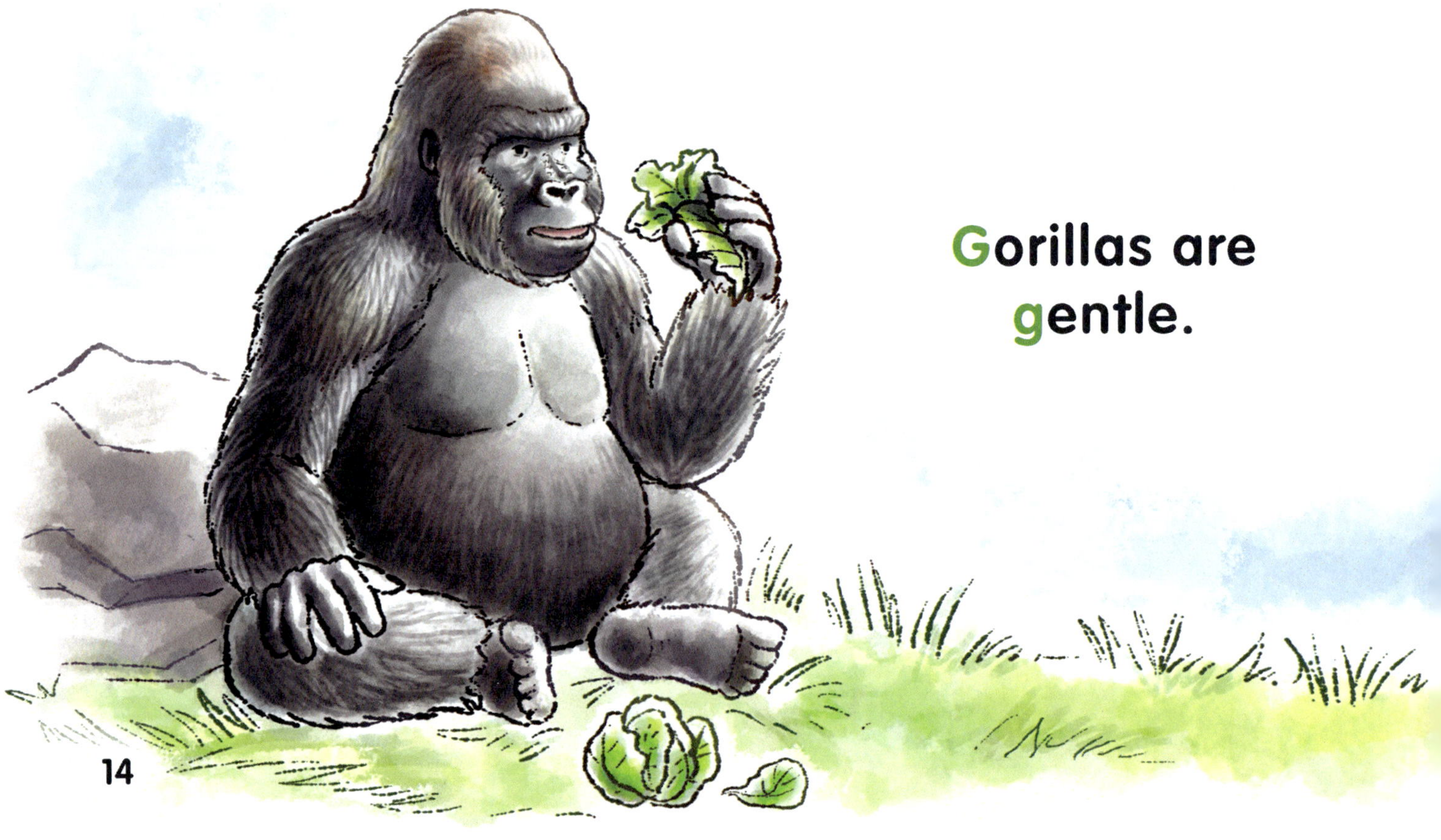

Gorillas are
gentle.

Where do baby gorillas sleep?

Hh

H is for hippopotamus

Hippos are heavy.

What do hippos eat?

Ii

I is for impala

Impalas are
intelligent.

Do all impalas have horns?

Jj

J is for jaguar

Jaguars have strong jaws.

How do jaguars clean their fur?

Kk

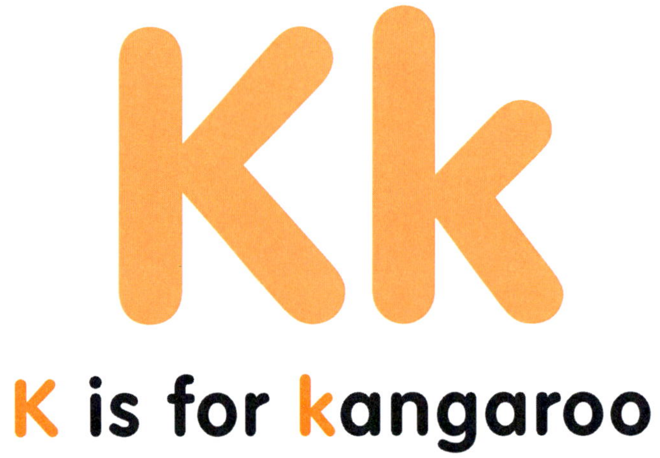

K is for kangaroo

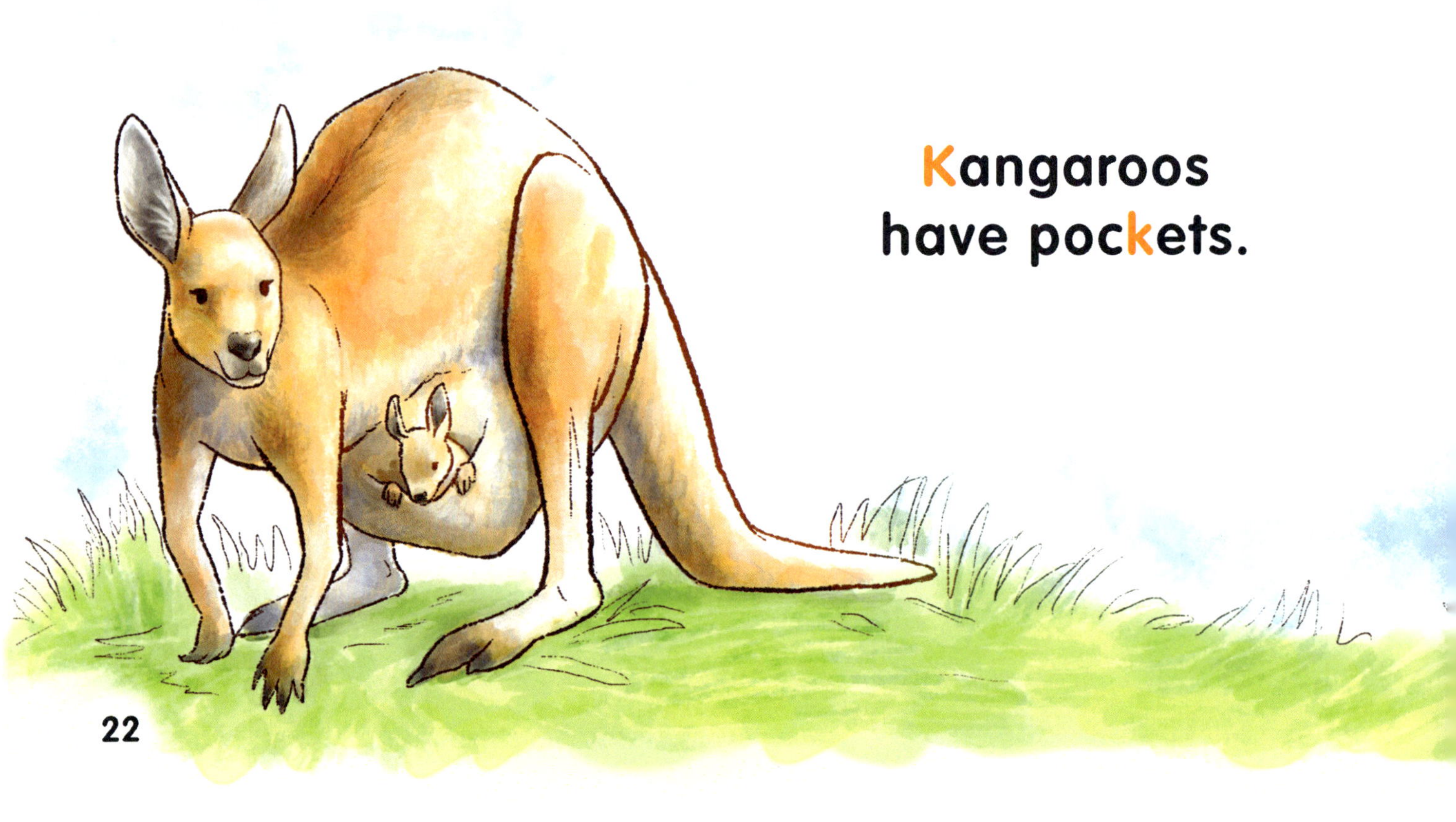

Kangaroos
have pockets.

What do you call a baby kangaroo?

Ll

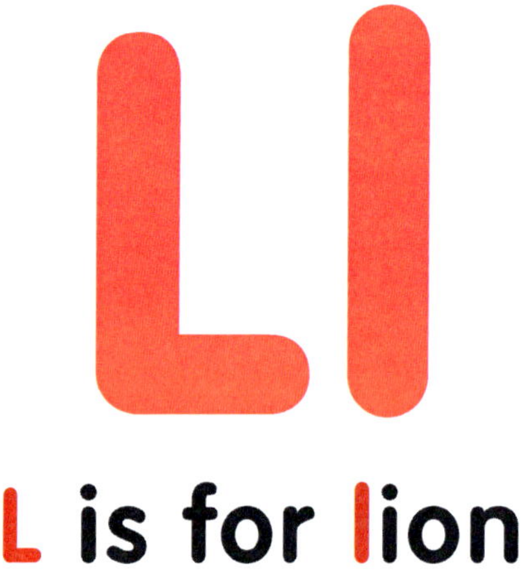

L is for lion

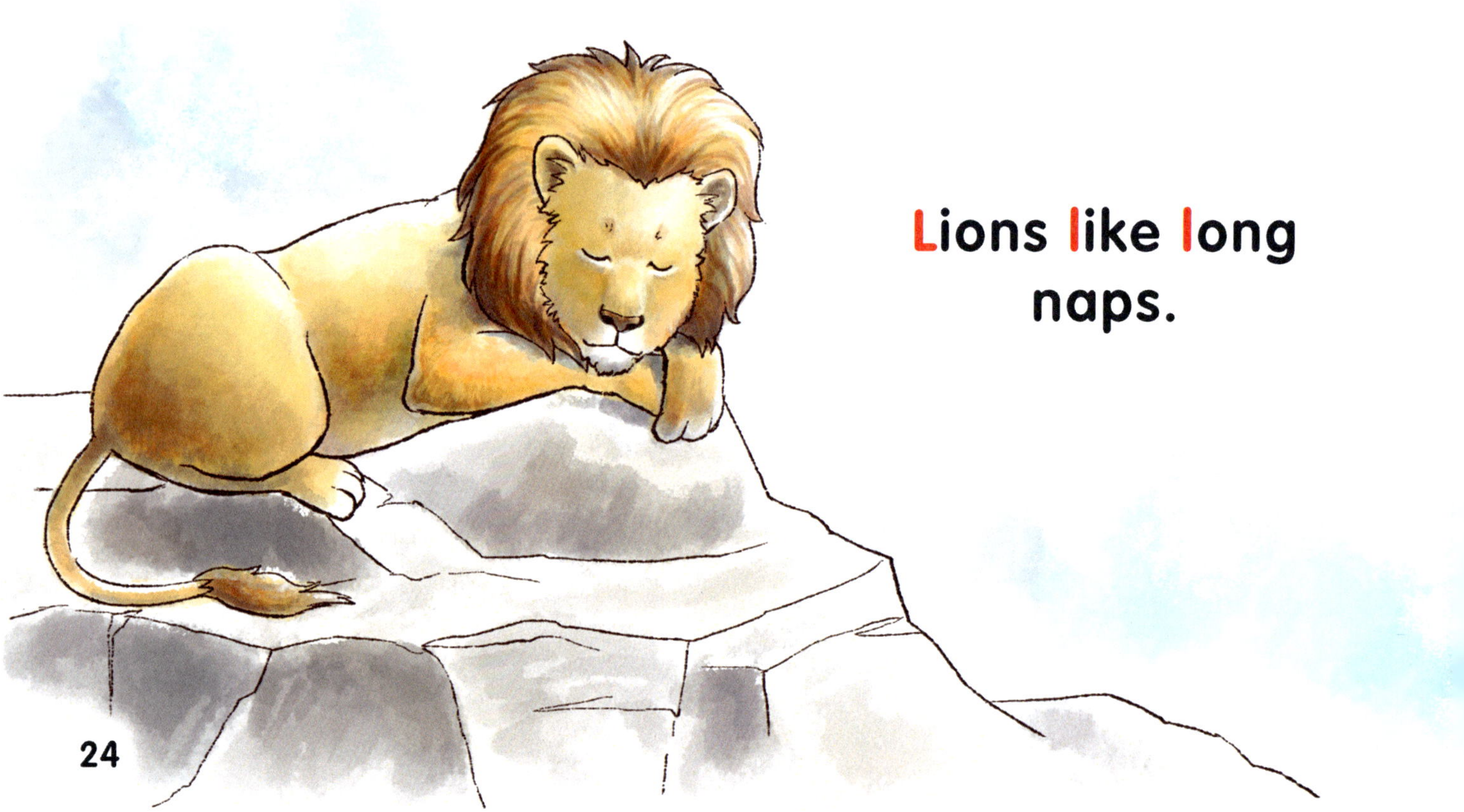

Lions like long naps.

What do you call a baby lion?

Mm

M is for monkey

Monkeys move very fast.

What do monkeys eat?

Nn

N is for nightingale

Nightingales lay eggs in nests.

When do nightingales sing?

Oo

O is for octopus

Octopuses live in the ocean.

What color is an octopus?

Pp

P is for panda

Pandas have paws.

What do pandas eat?

Qq

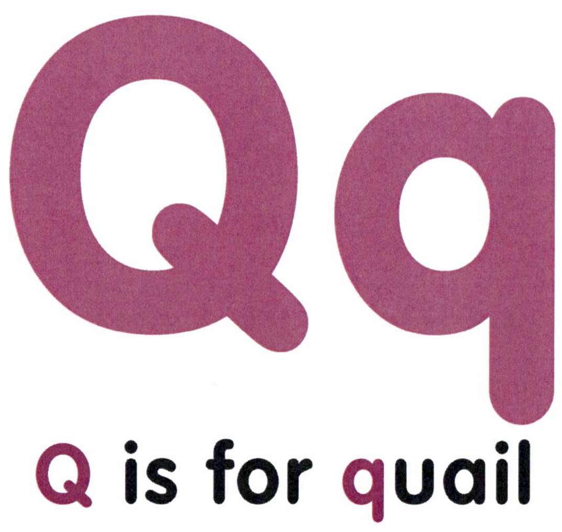

Q is for quail

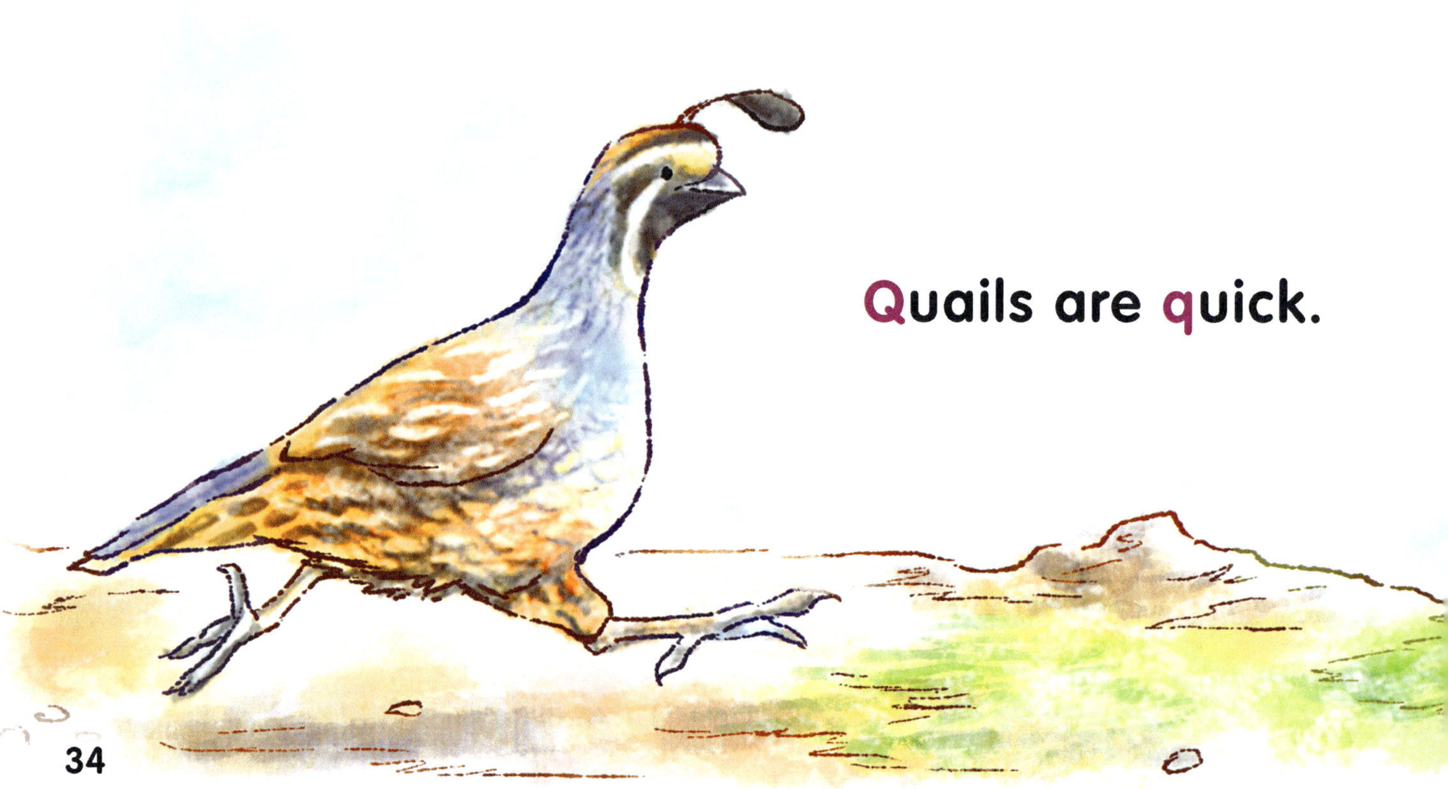

Quails are quick.

Can quails fly far?

Rr

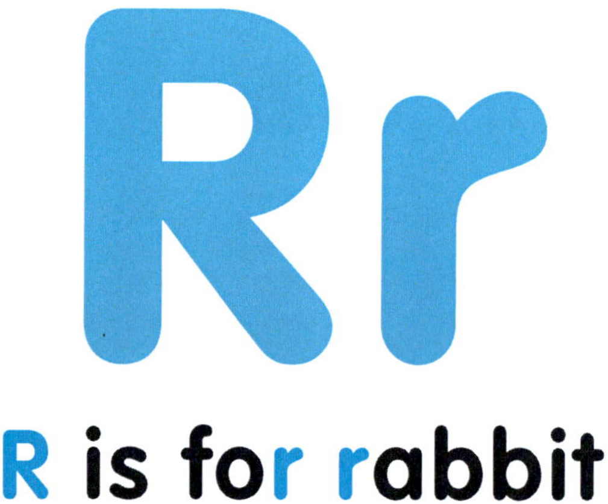

R is for rabbit

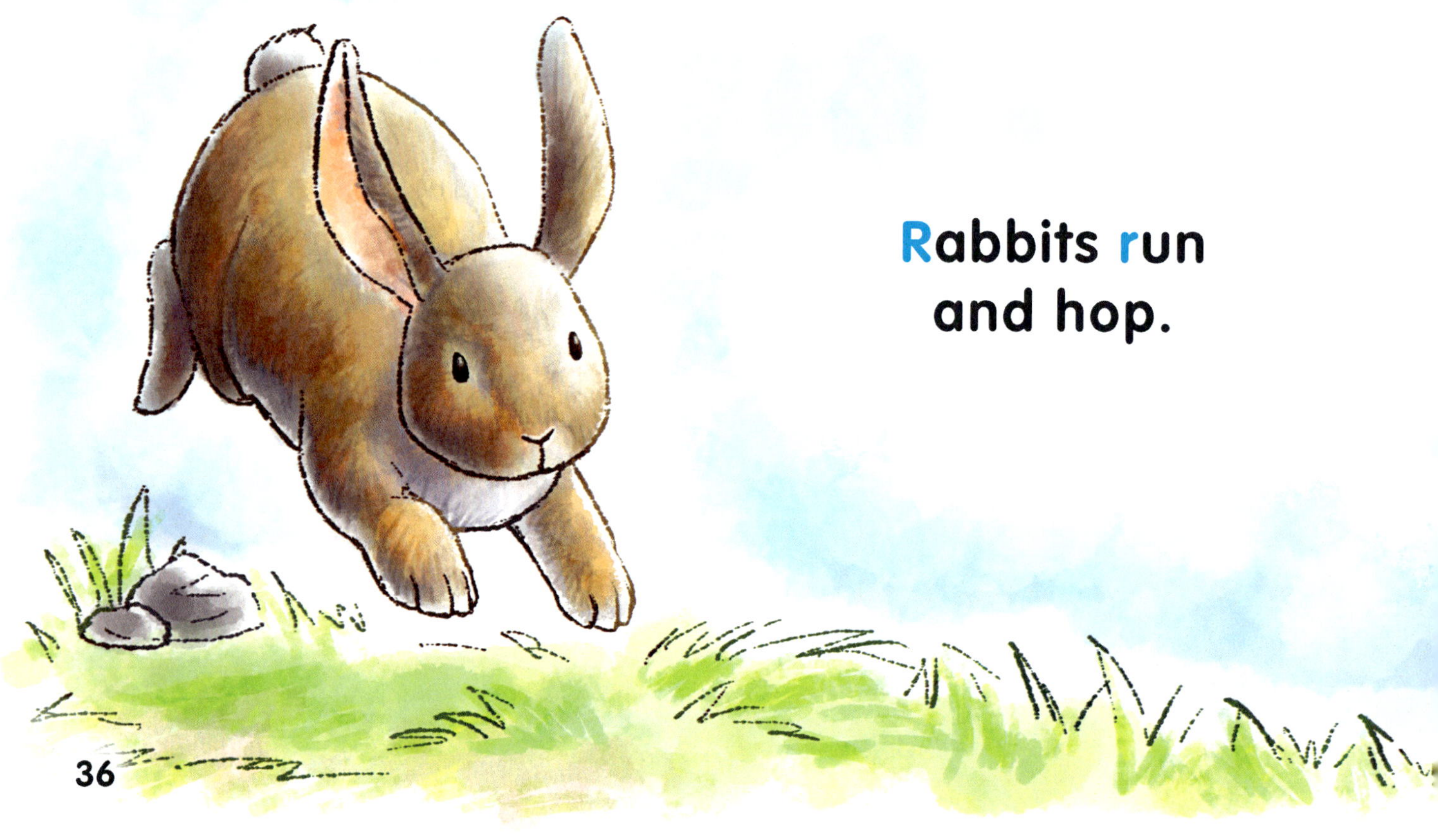

Rabbits run
and hop.

Where do rabbits sleep?

Ss

S is for sea lion

Sea lions are good swimmers.

Do sea lions live in the sea?

Tt

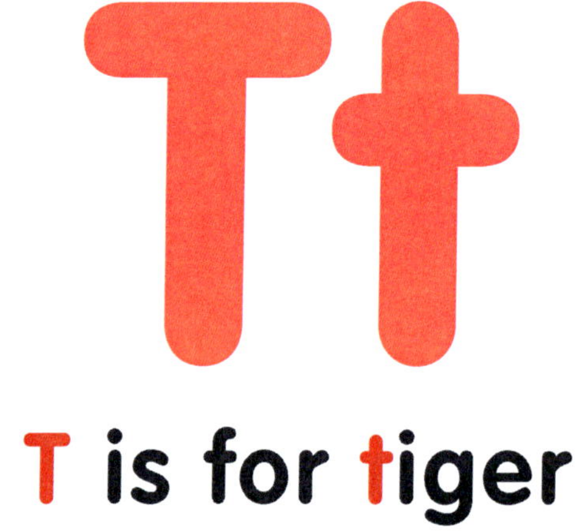

T is for tiger

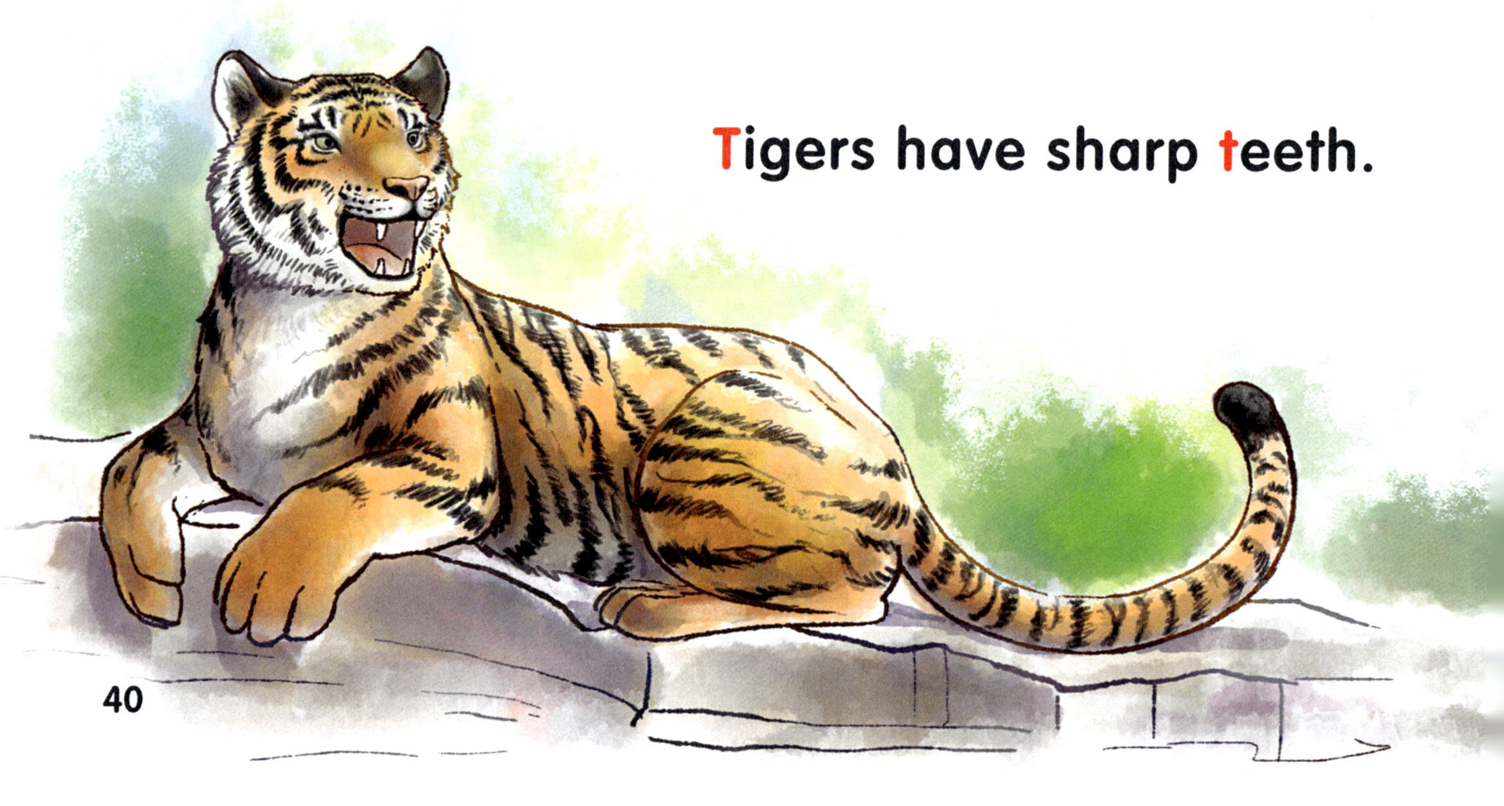

Tigers have sharp teeth.

Where do tigers live?

Uu

U is for umbrella bird

Umbrella birds fly
up in the sky.

Why do we call this bird an umbrella bird?

Vv

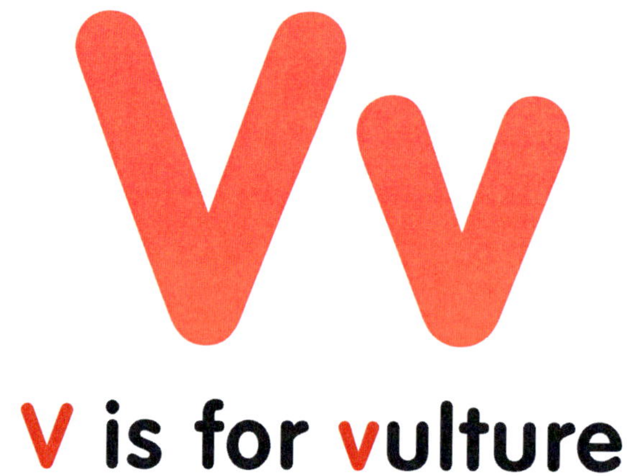

V is for vulture

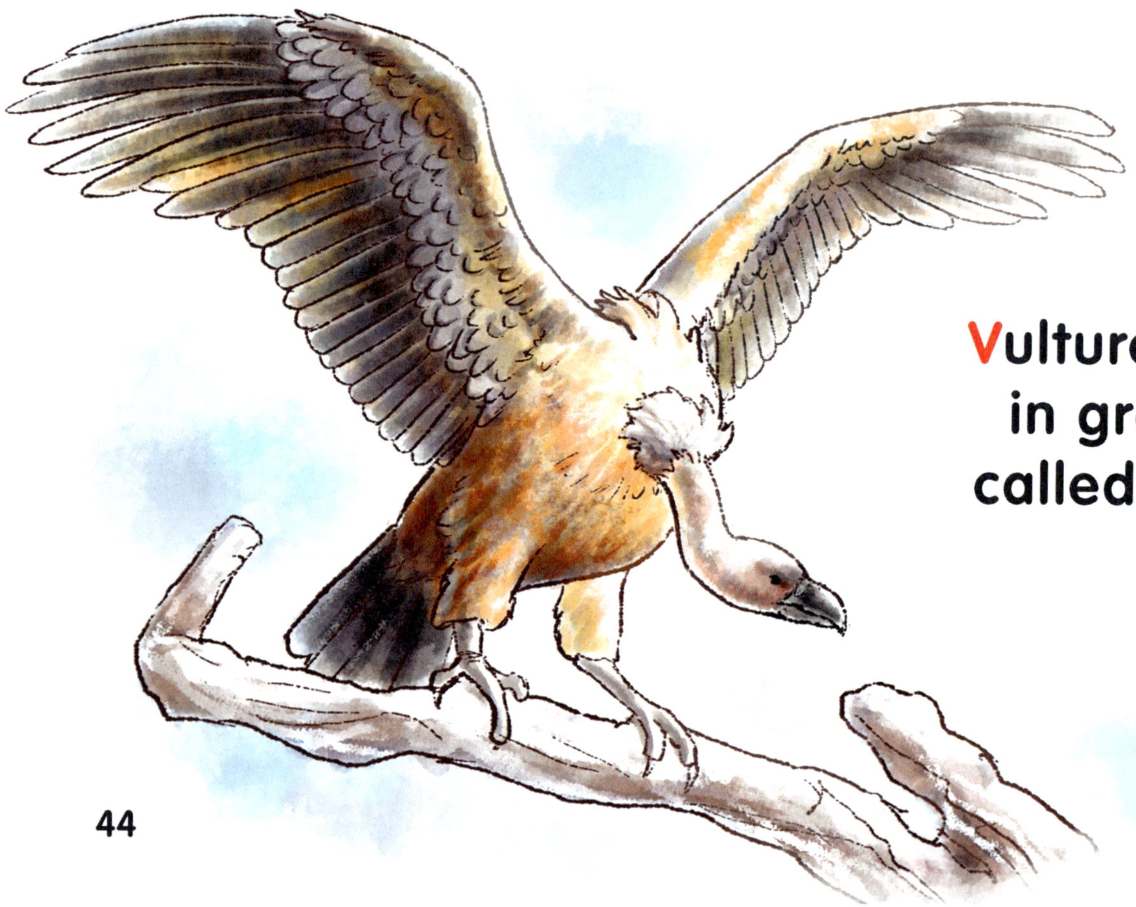

Vultures rest
in groups
called volts.

Do vultures have big wings?

Ww

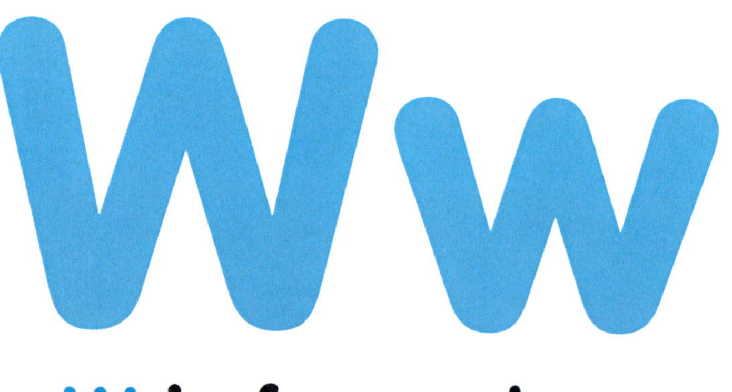

W is for walrus

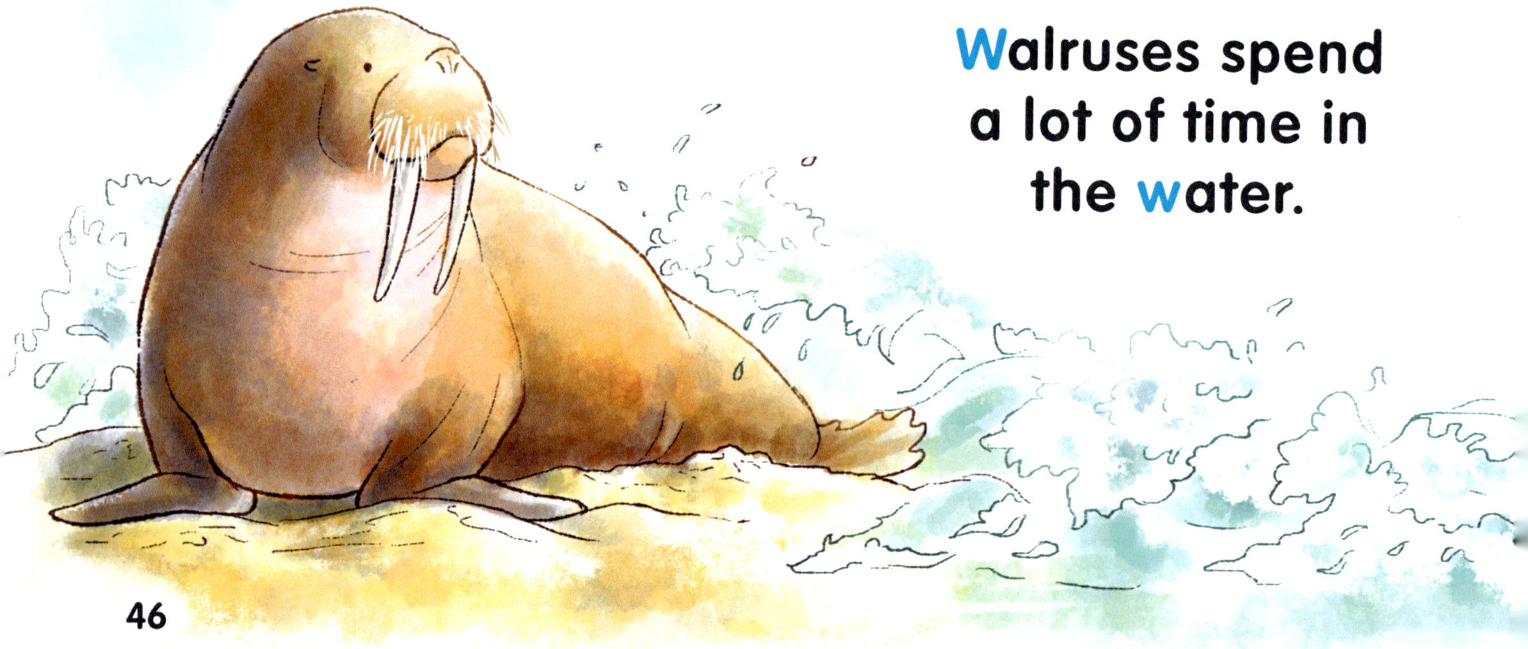

Walruses spend a lot of time in the water.

What are walrus tusks?

Xx

X is for x-ray fish

X-ray fish are extra colorful.

What do you call an x-ray fish baby?

Yy

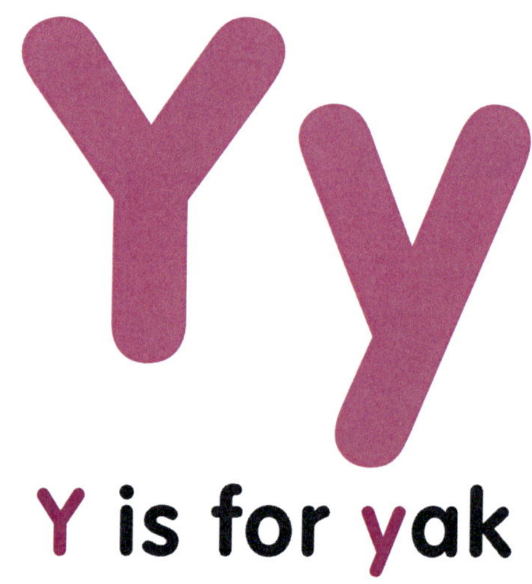

Y is for yak

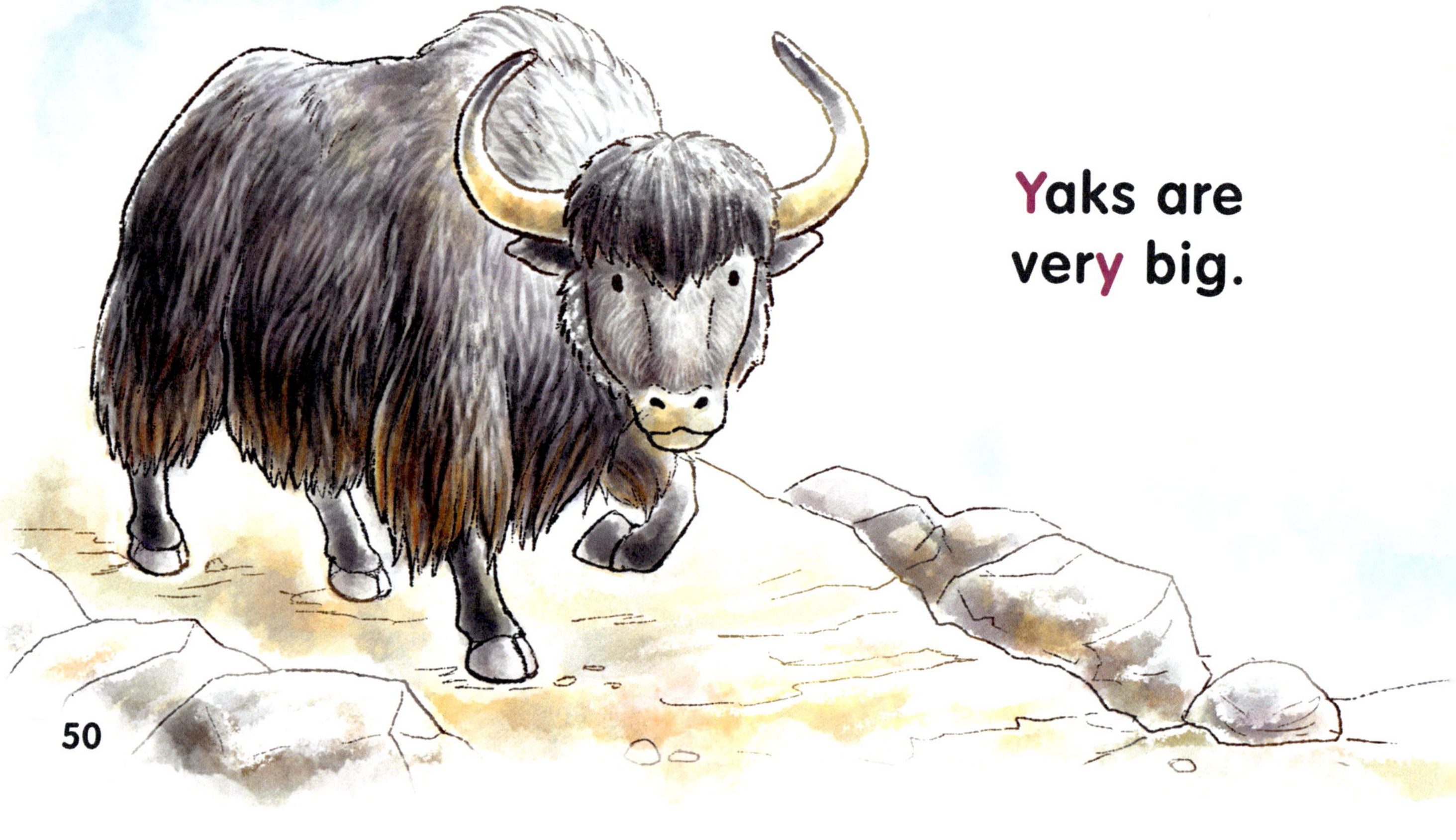

Yaks are
very big.

What do yaks eat?

Zz

Z is for zebra

Zebra stripes go
zig and zag.

Do all zebras have the same stripes?

Answers

Letter	Page	Answer
A	2	Alligators can swim and walk.
B	4	A baby bear is called a cub.
C	6	Cats lick themselves to keep clean.
D	8	A baby duck is called a duckling.
E	10	Elephants eat bushes, grass, fruits and other plants.
F	12	A baby fox is called a cub.
G	14	Gorilla babies sleep in nests with their mothers.
H	16	Hippos mainly eat grass.
I	18	Only male impalas have horns.[1]
J	20	Jaguars use their tongues to lick themselves clean.
K	22	A baby kangaroo is called a joey.
L	24	A baby lion is called a cub.
M	26	Monkeys eat plants, fruit, bugs and insects.

---

[1] If your child does not know what the word *male* means this is a good opportunity to explain to him or her that male means boys and men.

Letter	Page	Answer
N	28	Nightingales sing during the day and the night.
O	30	An octopus can be many colors including red, yellow, orange, brown and black.
P	32	Pandas love to eat bamboo.
Q	34	Quails do not fly long distances.
R	36	Rabbits sleep under the ground in holes called burrows.
S	38	Sea lions live on the land and in the sea.
T	40	Some tigers live in very warm places and others live in cold places.
U	42	When this bird spreads its feathers on top of its head, it looks like it has an umbrella up there!
V	44	Vultures have very wide wings and can fly very long distances.
W	46	Walrus tusks are long pointy teeth.
X	48	An x-ray fish baby is called a fry.
Y	50	Yaks mainly eat grass and other plants.
Z	52	Every zebra has its own set of stripes. No two zebras have exactly the same set of stripes.

Credits

Original Concept: William Newell

Author: Sarina Simon
Art Director: Oscar Camino
Illustrator: Satomi Asuy
Lead Programmer: Oscar Freyre
Programmer: Benjamin Mamani
Programmer: Carlos Duclós
Project Manager: Diego Fernández
Quality Assurance: Cecilia Martínez

And special thanks to: Antonny Argomedo, Jeancarlo Ascorra, Walter Barrantes, Javier Castillo, Eder Cépeda, Danny Chero, José L. Collantes, Franz Córdova, Carlos Custodio, Cesar García, Aldo Gianoli, Lionel Gonzales, Sergio Gonzales, Oscar Gutiérrez, Carlos Kohatsu, Jorge Miranda, José Napa, Claudia Okada, Herald Olivares, Hector Olivera, Fernando Paredes, Chiara Ridella, Paulo Rivas, Ronald Taipe, Pavel Tocto, Carlos Vásquez, Smith Vasquez, Jacqueline Vega, Mónica Verástegui, Mariela Yamamoto, Heidi Castro, and Alfredo Zorrilla.

Made in the USA
Lexington, KY
15 December 2017